Heidi & Daniel Howarth

What Makes Me Sad?

Sky Pony Press
New York

2

Little Polar Bear had never seen snow before.
He had felt it beneath his paws, felt it melt on the end of his nose, felt it cold on his tongue, but he had never seen it.

He was born surrounded by snow, in a snug
dark den, and now it was time to leave.
His mom dug with her powerful paws
and the bright light flooded in.

Little Polar Bear squinted. This light was
so bright.
All around, in every direction, it was white
and through bleary eyes, it was ever so bright.

It felt strange to be outside. His tummy felt nervous, his paws felt wobbly, and this snow was slippery.

He loved his warm dark den and
he was very sad to be leaving it.

"Why can't we stay here?" he asked Mommy Bear.
"We need food," said Mommy Bear, smiling, "and there is not a lot here."
Little Bear looked all around him. Mommy Bear was right.
There was nothing to eat.
Everywhere he looked, there was snow.

So they started to walk. The sun was high in the sky.
They walked and walked and walked.
When the sun finally dipped low enough in the sky
to look like it touched the ground, they stopped.
"Are we there yet?" asked Little Bear.
"No," replied Mommy Bear. "We still have a long way to go."

That night, as Little Bear
curled up close into Mommy
Bear's warm, soft fur, he
felt something again,
something deep
in his tummy. He
missed the cave.
He missed the
warmth and
the safety.

This new day had been cold, hard, and long. He really wanted to just go back home to his warm, dark, snowy den.

He stared at the bright moon in the sky and soon his eyelids felt heavy and he managed to fall asleep.

As they got nearer to the sea, the pack ice got thinner and thinner.
"Be careful," warned Mommy Bear.
"It is dangerous here. The ice is thin, but if we fall through, it will be difficult to get out or to swim."

She tried one more paw but the ice
was cracking.
Little Bear was very worried.
Mummy Bear smiled a kind smile.
"Watch me," she said.
Instead of placing her great big paw
on the ice and causing more cracks,
she slid onto her belly.

"What are you doing, Mommy?" asked Little Bear, laughing.
"You look funny."
"I am spreading my weight," replied Mommy Bear.
"Try it, it's fun."
Little Bear did so. Mommy Bear was right. It was fun.

The ice was now thicker again.
Little Bear was so hungry now, his tummy growled.
“Is it always so hard, Mommy?” he asked.

His mom looked very thoughtful
for some time before answering.

"There was a time when the ice stayed thick and strong. There were many seals to hunt and eat. But the air is warmer now. We have to travel further to find food."

"Our world is changing, so we have
to do what we can to survive in it.
When I look at you, I know we still have
a future." She smiled.
Her eyes were very sad, though.

"There is one thing that still fills me with joy, though."
And she smiled her warmest smile.
She opened her paws as wide as she could.
"Nothing makes me happier than a bear hug with
my wonderful cub."

What makes me feel sad

Not all stories or events in our life can be happy all the time. Sometimes things happen to us that make us sad. They are very difficult to understand.

The planet is warming up and the polar ice caps are melting. This is what this story is about.

Can the children think of a situation
that made them sad?
Now, can they think of something that
can always make them feel better?

What is the thing that makes
them most happy?
Is it a cuddle from Mom?
A game with their best friend?
Walking their dog?

Do the children know what the term
"carbon footprint" refers to?
Do they know that it refers to their
families' impact on the planet?

There is a lot we can do to help our planet. Encourage
the children to discuss recycling
and responsible energy use.

Can the children name any
"green technology?"
Have they heard of "wind farms,"
for example?

Our world is under a lot of pressure
at the moment.
Our climate is changing. Global warming
is changing the world very significantly
for some people and
also animals in our world.

Lots of things are thought to influence
the shift in our climate.
Can the children think of anything that could do this?
Here are some examples:
Air travel
Car journeys
Carbon fuels

What Makes Me Sad?

First Sky Pony Press Edition 2019.

10 9 8 7 6 5 4 3 2 1

Author: Heidi Howarth
Illustrations: Daniel Howarth
Design and layout: Gemser Publications, S.L.
Cover design: Mona Lin

Library of Congress Cataloging-in-Publication Data is available on file.

Print ISBN: 978-1-5107-4553-7
Ebook ISBN: 978-1-5107-4567-4

Printed in China